SOMEONE
FALLS
OVERBOARD
Talking through Poems

Stephen Kuusisto

Ralph James Savarese

Praise for *Someone Falls Overboard*

Who hasn't wanted to live that writer's dream, eavesdropping on two great poets? For nine days, Steven Kuusisto and Ralph Savarese exchanged poems, multiple poems daily, and responded to each one: riffing, sampling, griping, cracking wise. The result is *Someone Falls Overboard: Talking through Poems*, a project suggested by the poetic dialogue between William Stafford and Marvin Bell, but unmistakably Kuusisto and Savarese. Water runs through this book: a paradise, a poem-drinker, a physical place where the poets boat together, "Two disabled men—this isn't a joke," on Lake Winnipesaukee. Ultimately water becomes the current that pulls between two powerful and poetic intelligences. The project is as kinetic and un-precious as it sounds. "I've banished irony," writes Savarese, and Kuusisto responds, "Finnish underworld, a lake/where a swan glides." *Someone Falls Overboard* is crackling smart, hilarious without losing its urgency, centered firm in this historical moment yet an instant classic in the long tradition of poetry in conversation. Reading is listening, ear pressed against an irresistible door.— Susanne Paola Antonetta, author of *The Terrible Unlikelihood of Our Being Here*

Someone Falls Overboard is an effortless read and extremely funny! The poetic back-and-forth is brimming with wit, camaraderie and genuine emotion. It is an absolute treat, for us readers, to be in the audience as two good friends have a heartfelt conversation about themselves and everything in between. Savarese and Kuusisto have unlocked the secret to surviving a pandemic in style.—Siddharth Dhananjay, star of the film *Patti CAKE$*

Once in a great while, speed dating works. Something deep happens fast. So it is with *Overboard*, the rapid-fire exchange of two brilliant poets, Ralph James Savarese and Stephen Kuusisto. They go back and forth amid our current chaos and their own haunts like Ali and Frazier. It's jazz. It's chess. It's a repartee of reverence and irreverence. It's great.—Marty Dobrow, author of *Knocking on Heaven's Door: Six Minor Leaguers in Search of the Baseball Dream*

Written during the COVID-19 pandemic, *Someone Falls Overboard* is a poetic conversation and an answer to the isolation of lockdown. Tossing images and metaphors back and forth, riffing on each other's ideas, acclaimed writers Stephen Kuusisto and Ralph James Savarese explore the meaning of age, disability, poetry, and memory; what emerges is a single long poem about friendship, witty, inventive, profane.—George Estreich, author of *Fables and Futures: Biotechnology, Disability, and the Stories We Tell Ourselves*

A. R. Ammons once described two butterflies spiraling upward on each other's air currents as 'swifter in / ascent than they / can fly or fall' ('Trap'). And that's what's going on here with Kuusisto and Savarese, two masters of poetic improv soaring higher on each other's drafts than any artist could hope to fly alone. Witty and moving in equal parts, their collaboration makes for a can't-miss performance.—Julie Kane, author of *Mothers of Ireland: Poems*

To open this book is to remember that poetry is playtime—in the right hands. Kuusisito and Savarese goad each along in a game of 'look what you did, now look what I can do.' They create a series of interlocking playgrounds, and you never know who you might meet there, or where you might find yourself. There's George Eliot, Jay-Z, Jack Kennedy, Elizabeth Bishop. We're flying through the sky on an airplane, we wake up on an operating table, we're playing trombone like it's having sex. There's that kid peeing in the kiddie pool. Why is there shit on the church pew? Who's got diarrhea now? This pair of poets invites us into their intimate playground, a place where they express the tenderness of friendship in a vernacular lyricism that reminds us, in their words, 'We're smarter than we knew.'
—Jason Tougaw, author of *The One You Get: Portrait of a Family Organism*

Someone Falls Overboard is a back-and-forth between two poets that ranges from the goofy to the profound. The conversation is as far from the usual polished poetic fare as you can get; rather, it's interested in the raw ingredients—memory and association—and the ways in which seemingly disparate things can collide and intertwine. Strung loosely together, the poems are rough, fast, unpredictable, and very funny. It takes both recklessness and courage to play in public, but that's what these poets do, giving us a deep glimpse into a long friendship and demonstrating that 'You must / Get lost / To live.'—Chase Twichell, author of *Things as It Is*.

Nine Mile Books

Publisher: Nine Mile Art Corp.
Editors: Bob Herz, Stephen Kuusisto, Andrea Scarpino
Art Editor Emeritus: Whitney Daniels
Cover Art: "Liquor Peter & Jan," courtesy of the Collection of
Christopher B. Steiner
Cover design: Tilly Woodward
Nine Mile Books is an imprint of Nine Mile Art Corp

The publishers gratefully acknowledge support of the New York
State Council on the Arts with the support of Governor Andrew
M. Cuomo and the New York State Legislature. We also
acknowledge support of the County of Onondaga and CNY Arts
through the Tier Three Project Support Grant Program. We
have also received significant support from the Central New
York Community Foundation. This publication would not have
been possible without the generous support of these groups. We
are very grateful to them all.

ISBN: 978-1-7354463-5-6

Acknowledgements

We gratefully acknowledge the editors of the following journals in which some of these poems first appeared: *Hole in the Head Review, Main Street Rag, Months to Years, Mudlark, One Art, Red Wheelbarrow, 2River, Rogue Agent, The Haven*, and *Wordgathering*.

Contents

Introduction   18

I

In the Middle Distance... (SK)   23
Scoundrels (RJS)   24
Old Man's Verses Ride Again... (SK)   25
Arrow (RJS)   26
On Aging (SK)   27
Hem (RJS)   28
Cemetery... (SK)   29
Here Comes Santa Claus (RJS)   30
Christmas, 1963 (SK)   31
Naptime (RJS)   32
What's One to Make of the Relatives
       for God's Sake... (SK)   33
Welt (RJS)   34
I Like to Read About Love... (SK)   35
Hide and Weak (RJS)   36
The Swan of Tuonela (SK)   37
Samples (RJS)   38
A Lovely Native of Many Names... (SK)   39
Eggs (RJS)   40
Say What You Want No One's Much of a Poet... (SK)   41
Wet Pages (RJS)   42
A Pal of Mine... (SK)   43
Vessel (RJS)   44
Sunrise... (SK)   45
Picnickers (RJS)   46
I Like to Mimic Presidents... (SK)   47
Gait Coach (RJS)   48
Blind Travel, or, I Can't Explain It (SK)   49
Chin Up (RJS)   50

Euphemisms at Home (SK)   51
Yours (RJS)   52
From the Egyptian Book of the Dead... (SK)   53
COVID King (RJS)   54

II

I Visited a Gondola Repair Shop... (SK)   57
Roles (RJS)   58
Someone's Gone Out Fishing... (SK)   59
Extinguisher (RJS)   60
Born Three Months Early... (SK)   61
Rattle (RJS)   62
Lake District (SK)   63
Carriage (RJS)   64
When My Father Died... (SK)   65
Sandwich (RJS)   66
This Is How We Hold the Sky... (SK)   67
Tools (RJS)   68
Old Teachers... (SK)   69
Claw (RJS)   70
Spread the old poems across two tables... (SK)   71
Along the Mississippi (RJS)   72
I'm Old Enough (SK)   73
Swallow (RJS)   74
Notes for My Own Elegy... (SK)   75
Polyps (RJS)   76
Minatory Medicine (SK)   77
Two Kinds of Dead People (RJS)   78
Autumn (SK)   79
The Oldest Hackberry in Iowa City (RJS)   80
Mordant Grain (SK)   81
Oar (RJS)   82
9-11 (SK)   83
Iron (RJS)   84

Crows (SK)   85

Again (RJS)   86

Throat, Concluding with a Line from Livy (SK)   87

More to Me (RJS)   88

III

From a Lecture (SK)   91

Once When I Was Drunk (RJS)   92

Monster (SK)   93

Defaulted (RJS)   94

Getting Away with It (SK)   95

Underspin (RJS)   96

I Don't Care for Rilke (SK)   97

Spared (RJS)   98

You Can't Use the Word "Longing"
    in Poetry Anymore… (SK)   99

Gust (RJS)   100

Fuck Disney (SK)   101

Distinctions (RJS)   102

Of Course You Meant "Hung
    Like Harry Reems"… (SK)   103

He Wanted to Be on Broadway (RJS)   104

How It Is… (SK)   105

Gud (RJS)   106

More About Gud (SK)   107

Parishioners (RJS)   108

What Makes You Think… (SK)   109

Wet Monday (RJS)   110

One More Poem About Drinking in Foreign
    Locales (SK)   111

Broom (RJS)   112

When the statues come to life… (SK)   113

Theosophy (RJS)   114

Helena Petrovna… (SK)   115

There's More Dignity in Being a Terrorist (RJS)   116
Blind Reception 1966 (SK)   117
Housewife (RJS)   118
Lobster (SK)   119
Oh, No, DFW Again (RJS)   120
Trap (SK)   121
Ledge (RJS)   122

IV

Bag Man, Iowa City (SK)   125
Supernumerary (RJS)   126
Now and then... (SK)   127
At the Movies (RJS)   128
You have to choose... (SK)   129
Heehawing (RJS)   130
Leaves blow through the halls.... (SK)   131
The Problem with Mythology (RJS)   132
The World Before Eclairs or Odysseus (SK)   133
1990 (RJS)   134
Peloponnese Taverna 1977 (SK)   135
Riser (RJS)   136
Pup Canto (SK)   137
Lohemann's (RJS)   138
Jordan Marsh, etc. (SK)   139
Profound (RJS)   140
From the Greek (SK)   141
Due (RJS)   142
Tinker Bell (SK)   143
Wings (RJS)   144
Admission (SK)   145
The Anti-Vaxxers Are at It Again (RJS)   146
Pass the Plasma, Dolley Madison (SK)   147
Fists (RJS)   148
Fists or Cake (SK)   149

Vespucci (RJS)   150
Cibo (SK)   151
Give Passion Its Due (RJS)   152
What If (SK)   153
Spoons (RJS)   154
More About Spoons (SK)   155
Angel (RJS)   156

Biographies   158

In memory of Marvin Bell

I pinch off
a part of the story I know;
toss it to you.
—Marvin Bell, *Segues*

The forest answers
in the same way
one shouts at it.
—Finnish saying

With old men
and flowering cabbages,
there is nothing left to do.
—Sicilian saying

Introduction

When Marvin Bell and William Stafford published a collection of poems titled *Segues* in 1983, I was instantly smitten. Two long-time friends, both acclaimed poets, had taken it upon themselves to write poems to each other and frame both a literary correspondence and the good-natured play of poetry writing as a shared challenge. That they were notable teachers of creative writing and familiar with giving students "prompts"— assignments designed to spur the imagination—may have influenced them initially, but it's the book's growing affection and conversant ease that still strikes one after all these years.

I wondered if I could have a segue with my friend Ralph James Savarese, a poet and disability studies scholar who teaches at Grinnell College and lives in Iowa City. I live far from him in upstate New York. We are both disabled. I'm blind, and navigating in public during the COVID-19 pandemic is terrifying; watching good friends suffer and fall ill is equally frightening. Ralph has a serious auto-immune condition and the sight of maskless college students congregating just outside his door has been for him a daily reminder of how mortal we are and how inexpressibly dear life is.

Grousing over the phone, I said, "What if we were to write a sequence of poems back and forth as Marvin and Bill did back in the day?" The aim would be to think less of the stateliness poems often partake of in favor of quickness, candor, and the sparks the imagination tends to throw when working fast and under duress.

The epistolary renga that emerges is vulgar, learned, elegant, wildly irritable, mournful, sloppy, nostalgic and sling-shotted with ironies.

—SK

The more estranged we become from one another in these COVID times, the more art needs to infiltrate life—not step to the side of, and reflect, on it. A traditional sense of craft feels especially lonely now and inadequate. It achieves its remove at a price. The prisoners—us!—need hourly letters; the patients—us! —need minutely medicine. Build the bridge as you cross it! Girder after girder, step after step.

Or to change the metaphor, imagine if while struggling in the water you had to paint your life preserver, if decoration made it float. Imagine the water as a keyboard, the flailing of arms as type. Writing as a constant, a practice, the next breath—not something that comes of breath or for which lungs are merely the prerequisite. The lungs themselves.

Steve would send a poem at 7:00 a.m. (6:00 a.m. my time), and 12 hours later, we'd have breathed out 6 poems collectively, 3 a piece—or on a good day, one that really panted, 8 poems, 4 a piece. Each in response to the one before it. *How* they responded varied considerably, and that was half the fun. The challenge, like the pandemic itself, required invention and elasticity. Only connect!

—RJS

I

In the Middle Distance... (SK)

Does anyone read Louis Simpson anymore? Is it time
for a smoke? How about Robert Hayden?
Where do the poets go—please
say Valhalla, among the living they're not read,
though I can see them through a glass
and others—Ignatow, Rukeyser,
Thomas McGrath, my old teacher
Don Justice…the living now
read clean menus and phones.
The poets born early last century
had fatigued and ruined hearts,
which should not be forgotten,
for some God truly looked down upon them.
I want to stare a little while,
blind though I am,
as Hart Crane lifts his heavy arms.

Scoundrels (RJS)

They used to say of a father
who left: *He went out for a smoke*
and never came back.
Translation: *The fucker abandoned*
us; he didn't leave a dime.
It's the same with poets:
every reader is a child
and every poem, a betrayal.
The word moves on.
Truth is, we nagged
them to death.
Books are like milk bottles:
they wait to be opened
and spoil quickly.
We're all just scoundrels
of the moment.

Old Man's Verses Ride Again… (SK)

1580s, *skowndrell*, of unknown origin,
though my great grandfather was a wheelwright
who'd build a sleigh
or a child's coffin "out there"
in Finland.
It's thought to come
from Anglo-French *escoundre*
"to hide oneself" (the meaning of work).
In the good old days,
when you'd be tempted
to curl up in a newly completed box,
cat-like just to see
if you'd fit,
then as now
it meant getting away with it.
You'd find a way to fit.

Arrow (RJS)

I remember wanting a suit
three sizes too big.
I thought shoulders might give
a sense of purpose.
I thought *man* was something
that arrived like a taxi—
you could summon it.
I had confidence in spades.

In college, I dug graves for a priest
until he found me
weeping over a stone.
The word *sin* can be traced back to archery.
In the Book of Judges,
the Benjaminites were so good
with their bows they could
aim at a hair and not *chait*.

I still miss my father.

On Aging (SK)

Any minute
the man will arrive,
Senex who sees things
upside down,
drinks oak leaf wine,
advertises his faith in cold,
but not now…
"Pretend you're not ancient,"
said my shrink
when I said,
"I get enough exercise
just pushing my luck."
I didn't tell her King Charles II
hid from the Roundheads
in a large oak at Boscobel
or how staying still is the work of the skull.

Hem (RJS)

Economists speak of leisure,
the work of sculls, which
disturb the water about as much
as language disturbs the mind.
Saturday morning: you enter
like a surgeon or like Moses
parting the red sun.
With your face to the past,
only the coxswain
worries about what's ahead.
Angelus Novus, little boat servant,
light as a feather.
While he gets a free lunch,
you're threading a needle.
It's enough exercise to scare your wife.
Your heart wants a new hem.

Cemetery... (SK)

I love apostates: Marx, Ingmar Bergman...
Once in Highgate I saw hundreds
of sunken tombs erected
for my kind—my kind—
those who, alive, floated
in blue kiddie pools
of longing, then climbed out.
Funny though, so many
of the graves
stood in watery places,
George Eliot's, awash
in grass, Beatrix Potter,
Godless mother who
preferred mushrooms
to bibles—there she was
surrounded by well-behaved fungi.

Here Comes Santa Claus (RJS)

As a kid I'd urinate in the kiddie pool—
there was no lid, and the opening
seemed large enough to relax me.
I didn't have to steer or direct—
my penis wasn't the least bit
like a teacher's punishing finger.
Rather, it was the tail of a bull
in the ring. Or a horseman's whip.
Or a kite string lifting me
out of sadness.
The withholding sort,
skinny as a reed, I oncerefused to poop for two weeks,
thought I could gain weight this way.
Freud called shit a child's first gift.
Oh, how I hated Christmas!

Christmas, 1963 (SK)

It was I killed Jack Kennedy, blind kid
with telescopes
fitted over glasses—
"You're Oswald," said a boy named Touhey.
Odd how I believed him.
It was I who aimed
and fired—who saw
so little, who saw grey,
who saw others
only with imagination,
who couldn't see a chalkboard
but knew how to kill.
Or if I didn't,
knew the game
involved me
even from my corner
of the pool.

Naptime (RJS)

My maternal grandmother
was the maid, and my maternal
grandfather the chauffeur,
for the Bouvier family.
When found in a closet together,
they were fired—let go like balloons
or like dogs in heat. The former
became a cleaning lady
who died at 60 on her knees;
the latter, a cab driver who was
paralyzed in a traffic accident.
Another cab pushed him right
into a department store.
The mannequins, suddenly
prostrate, looked asleep.
Call it *Naptime for Dummies*.

What's One to Make of the Relatives for God's Sake... (SK)

Tragic as us but with bigger stages,
victrolas, dynamite, motorcars,
my mother's father put TNT in gin,
lost fingers to blasting caps,
bought houses to destroy them,
wandered about in a raccoon coat,
wore diamond stickpins—
all without vanity.
America has lots of forests
and vainglorious types.
Stay out of them,
though grandpa taught
my mother at 8
to shoot first
and ask questions later
before leaving her alone for days.

Welt (RJS)

It's funny how siblings will allow
one child to be beaten.
At least it's not me...
Funny how love is all about distinction:
this, not that; her, not him.
Funny how unfunny it all is.
A welt is wellness to a "t."
A welt is Loch Ness to a lake.
Monster, please come devour me.
I survived a cracked skull—
"I fell," I told the doctor—
and my son survived three
drownings in a bath.
Alone for days in a closet,
he made friends with his
foster mother's clothes.

I Like to Read about Love… (SK)

Once I hid inside a piano
when quite small.
There was violence
in childhood,
and grown I see how each story
disciplines my heart.
How I love Tristan and Isolde:
their joy was one thing,
their fate grim and brutal—
the coarseness
and farces of lovers
who lived as we did
when girls and boys
in the wild hills.
We heard lies on the wind,
so moved out of sight.

Hide and Weak (RJS)

I've banished irony,
taken away its citizenship,
sold its umpteen houses,
and it just laughs.
"You need me more
than I need you.
I'm like your phone
or refrigerator."

If love is a peach,
then this poem is the pit.
"See what I mean?
You're addicted to me.
Do away with the sun
and lose your shadow."
A Trappist monk will say
just two words in a month:

"I'm hungry."

The Swan of Tuonela (SK)

Finnish underworld, a lake
where a swan glides
in perfect silence,
weakness like coins,
useless—"Hello,"
I said to a monk
in the sauna at Velamo.
100 years old
he was. Understand
he'd carried icons
out of Russia
across the ice,
so frailty
was sidelong,
unreal,
like Mary's tears.

Samples (RJS)

That time on a train
from Warsaw to Gdansk,
a Finnish man,
having sat down
in our compartment,
opened his
mirrored briefcase:
so many different kinds of vodka,
so many colors—
like stained glass
or paint samples for the throat.
"Holy Water," he said
in leaky Polish,
and as we passed a church
shaped like a ship,
"Keeps you afloat."

A Lovely Native of Many Names... (SK)

I can count backwards the way they like
in the hospital by sevens, and this morning
by touch I identified a wind blown
leaf—Amelanchier—service berry,
and it's going to rain.
The day is dark.
I think Wallace Stevens
saw Bishop Berkeley
in a light bulb,
which was almost
innocent.
Mind over matter
until dull clots
have their revenge.
Let the lamp affix its beam.
Shine here...

Eggs (RJS)

Can I say it?
Miłosz wasn't much
of a poet.
All bombast and wings,
a kind of preachy pterodactyl.
A ship anchor
floats better than
his verses.
Now Herbert, on the other hand,
or Szymborska—
shy little robin's eggs
ever so happy not to hatch.
A basket,
Easter morning,
Easter moaning.
Make me an omelet, please.

Say What You Want No One's Much of a Poet... (SK)

I was reading Elizabeth Bishop
beside a lake when the book
fell in. I watched it sink,
pictured it spiraling
and fish
with isinglass eyes
drifting past.
I thought it important
to remember
the last lines I'd read:
A moose has come out of
the impenetrable wood
and stands there, looms, rather,
in the middle of the road.
I gathered my oars—
"She was better than this—wasn't she?"

Wet Pages (RJS)

Stop throwing your children
in the water, Steve!
Everything sinks,
including these lines,
which fish for hope.
If I read one more story
about the pandemic…
My teacher had polio;
his son, who wore a cape
in the movies, fell off a horse
and couldn't move.
It took him a while
to want to live.
What nerve titling
a book *Still Me*.
That pun is a moose.

A Pal of Mine… (SK)

who lives in the far north
saw homeless men in snow,
each holding his loaf of French bread
and a plastic bottle of anti-freeze.
Their trick was to hollow out the loaves,
pour the liquid through
and drink it
from emptied crust.
"You won't go blind
this way," one said,
adding, "you won't…"
You know me, Ralph,
I'm Episcopalian—
Lord, may we be living vessels
of mercy, grace, and love.
Remind us to carry our treasure gingerly…

Vessel (RJS)

Two disabled men—this isn't a joke—
take a boat out onto Lake Winnipesaukee.
One is blind; the other has heart
rot and crumbled joints.
But first the latter must take
a test at the fly-and-tackle shop.
Though he's read *Moby-Dick*
a hundred times—it's his Bible—
he doesn't know what the word *aft* means.
First question: Someone falls overboard.
Should you a) rev the motor and move in circles
around them or b) wait until Jesus descends?
Obviously b. a uses up too much gas!
Out on the lake, they moon
the Republican nominee.
Mormon Mitt has a humble mansion.

Sunrise... (SK)

My mother when a girl
stepped from a boat
to walk on lilies
so perfect.
I am looking for you, Captain...
The algebra of waters
sets loose the gorging
of green things,
as she'd say,
were she still with us.
Boats are somber,
hollow affairs.
Inside death,
even when we pretend
otherwise,
is there another place?

Picnickers (RJS)

Coming into Wolfboro, I panicked,
and you took the wheel.
It was like parallel parking on a hill
in Vermont except the boats were all
dancing drunk or having a seizure.
I thought echolocation was a myth!
But there you were, throwing
your voice like a baseball.
The Tom Seaver of accents:
William F. Buckley, Dutch…
Even then, you made me laugh
and docked the god damn whaler.
When you climbed out—
your guide dog, Nira, leading you—
two picnickers gasped.
Who needs eyes or math?

Just listen to your own voice.

I Like to Mimic Presidents... (SK)

The world is too much with us—
I "do" Reagan
in the Motor Vehicle Department,
asking strangers
in "the Gipper's" voice
if they like Campbell's soup.
Or Bill Clinton
at the Sonic
wants to know
if you understand
you look like Dmitri Shostakovich,
and are you going to eat
those French Fries?
Danger! Nixon
in the hardware store asks
if you know what to do with tiny screws.

Gait Coach (RJS)

After my hip replacement—
I remember looking
at the x-rays
and being fascinated
by the tiny screws—
I had to learn how
to walk again,
to find myself in legs.
Crutches, walker, cane…
The gait coach said,
"Movement is like
a foreign language:
you must live there
to learn it." And so,
my feet moved to Venice
and my knees, to Milan.

Blind Travel, or I Can't Explain It (SK)

I managed to get lost in Venice,
just me and my dog.
In Milan I went in circles.
How troublesome the streets!
We manage,
talk to ourselves,
mumble mumble death
just there; psst,
can't find our way
back to the Bridge of Sighs.
I knew a man
who made his living
manufacturing odors
for vacuum packed foods —
lost, I swear he follows me.

Chin Up (RJS)

Now that's a euphemism.
Manufacturing odors, my ass!
Exactly. As a boy, I longed
to play the trombone,
but my mother said "no."
"That instrument's too sexual.
The arm movements, the lips—
Good God! We all know what
'the saints go marching in' means."
Yet I persisted: I found a way
that was much more organic,
though equally puckered.
Mozart was my guide:
By the love of your skin,
I shit on your nose
so it runs down your chin.

Euphemisms at Home (SK)

"Don't drag your ass in the sand"
was a favorite; "mercy filling,"
a drink in time; "hang glide,"
too long in the can.
Being sad or talented
could hurt you
in all the wrong places.
Scandinavian
cruelty, so Lutheran,
everyone throwing ink wells
at the Devil.
People come out of church,
converse about the sermon,
sniff at the autumn air.
The stalks of the potato plants
rotting fast this year...

Yours (RJS)

Yes, I'm infantile. And you?
My professor friends want to be taken
seriously. As if they were kids
and life were a kidnapping.
A reputation is a dungeon,
which you enter willingly.
DO NOT BLAME THE VICTIM!
We live in all of the wrong places.
The right ones mock us: Amber Alert!
(Metaphor, the last refuge of a scoundrel.)
Last night, showing my age,
I screamed at the college kids
in the rental next door:
"Turn down your fucking music."
It was 2:00 a.m. Wife-beater
and boxers. Nobel, I'm yours!

From the Egyptian Book of the Dead... (SK)

The hieroglyphs representing humans
or animals were left incomplete
or drawn mutilated,
most likely to prevent them
causing any harm to the dead pharaoh.
Yes, Pharaoh so sweet,
with his honey packed ears,
his eyelashes
dusted with assassin bugs,
insects dressed as ash,
lying in wait for
anything that moved.
Well, it's safe.
The king never starved,
but neither
was he rescued...

COVID King (RJS)

Do no harm, says
the Hippocratic oaf.
Pharaoh's doctor believes
in death, just not his.
I wrote a book about
our murder hornet,
and he's still as orange
and as lethal as ever.
Turd immunity! Let the virus
sting-fuck every American.
Trumpty Dumpty
fat on a pall,
Trumpty Dumpty's
penis is small.
An insect lands on
the White House lawn.

II

I Visited a Gondola Repair Shop... (SK)

With my guide dog—a first,
they said—then "on"
to Harry's for martinis,
blind guy
at Orson's table,
by jinky wave your dinky!
(Welles ate five trays
of shrimp toast
while Hemingway
wrote "The Green Hills of Africa"
upstairs.) Outside,
pickpockets waited.
Drinking to success...
Iron prow-heads of the gondolas,
called "fero da prorà"
lay everywhere on the floor.

Roles (RJS)

They had roomed together at Julliard, Clark and Mork,
the 6 foot 4 "studly of studlies" and the 5 foot 10 "little fool
    ferret boy."
When Chris lay in a hospital bed, Robin showed up in scrubs
and with a Russian accent said, "I'm the proctologist.
I need to perform an examination." "I knew then,"
Chris later wrote, "if I could laugh, I could live."
They had studied with the great John Houseman,
a Welles collaborator, famous for his role in *The Paper Chase*.
They've all now gone the way of judgments and funerals.
My teacher, too, Chris's dad, and Dana, Chris's wife.
"Escape the cape," the actor told himself, having been typecast.
In Guatemala, a skeletal folk saint named San Pascualito
appears with a scythe, cape, and crown: he's *King of the
    Graveyard!*
Every now and again, he cures diseases. I say get to work
on full paralysis and lewy body dementia. In my mind,
this poem goes on and on: it's like an actor beseeching

a ghost off-stage—call her the muse—"Lines, please."

Someone's Gone Out Fishing... (SK)

A friend who drove a taxi
in Manhattan picked up
Mel Torme, "the velvet fog"
who sang "The Folks Who Live on the Hill."
But there were no hills
on Fifth Avenue.
And once upon a time,
I sat next to Judy Collins
while flying—but never
let on I knew.
Tragedy is all around,
restless like a Sumerian vowel,
finding the nearest death,
as sounds do,
the ones from our throats,
from the very back...

Extinguisher (RJS)

Send in anything but clowns.
That irony is overwrought,
and the makeup gets all over everything.
I've run out of tears—
at least performative ones.
Will soon run out of jokes.
How do my friends stomach me?
With a vent hood, says my wife.
I'm a constant grease fire on the stove.
Do you want something fried?
Your shoes, perhaps?
Just add chili sauce and stir.
It's raining acrobats today.
They fall like snow in summer
and rise like mist in spring.
Timing is overrated.

Born Three Months Early... (SK)

Even today I show up early.
My brother, my twin,
who didn't make it,
he shows up early, too.
He's in heat pipes.
He's frost on the pond.
That first ice
looks like an illness
on a face,
though there's nothing
wrong with disfigurement.
Everyone says so:
it's too soon.
Set the clocks back,
William, don't forget me.
We've still got an hour.

Rattle (RJS)

The
drowned
live
in
radiators—
that's
why
you
must
fill
them
with
water.
The
radiators,
I

mean.

Lake District (SK)

Let me say something
about my lute:
it's made from a birch,
which, as you know,
isn't always a musical tree.
Birches grow
by serendipity
in marsh land—
tall, thin mistakes.
This is my instrument
then, this thing
making music
from nature's unseemly muddle.
Don't say what you mean
when you're first in love
shaking your hair.

Carriage (RJS)

So shallow rooted,
birch trees make fun of place,
even as they cry, "Beauty! Beauty!"
Even as they decay like baby teeth.
In Frost's poem "Home Burial,"
the husband says, "Three foggy mornings
and one rainy day will rot the best
birch fence a man can build."
Facts are terrible things,
uncaring, indifferent.
Husbands, too—or maybe not.
Maybe reason is just a form of Novocaine.
When my nephew Charlie died,
my sister-in-law pushed him around
the neighborhood for hours:
an infant, lute-like, in its case,

in its carriage…

When My Father Died... (SK)

We drove his ashes to the cemetery
only to find we'd forgotten
to hire a priest—"we"...
that's when everyone stepped back,
leaving me beside the hole.
"You're the poet," someone said.
I could climb down with him
or speak. I do not know
what this kind of loving is,
this calling of image,
this eros of lines remembered,
but it was Walt
came then—
nothing collapses,
and to die is different from
what any one supposed, and luckier.

Sandwich (RJS)

Poets are
like people
who join
the army:
there's nothing
voluntary about
it. Family
spurn our
words until
death digs
a hole
in their
eyes—until
dinner is
a dirt
sandwich. Let's

get Mikey...

This Is How We Hold the Sky... (SK)

Whichever way we move
is ours—even shadows tell—
mute loving, glass,
wood for new rooms,
men repeating their turns,
hammering
first the abstract,
then the good,
which is how air
and tools
become us,
though saying it
isn't wise
in some circles
where people
talk a lot.

Tools (RJS)

In Memoriam F.D. Reeve

Like five renaissance men or one Archimedes—
my teacher, Franklin. A steel-backed piano,
as upright as any Christian, in front of which
my wife, in childhood, had sat like a POW
and would now sit, a young, married woman
wanting to make amends with music (she'd soon
share a teacher with Solzhenitsyn's son, Igor;
my teacher had translated the old man's
Nobel Address)—that piano had just gone through
the back deck, her mother having kindly sent it
from Cleveland. When I called, he said, "I'm on my way."
An hour later, a tree and a pulley had extracted it
like a tooth. You should have seen it swaying
in the wind. Drunken notes, birch ivory blues…
The thing weighed 800 stone, made grooves
in the floor. My gratitude was just as ponderous—

and so later was my grief.

Old Teachers… (SK)

That I loved them
was indisputable.
That I didn't
love myself
is a story so old
even Archimedes' neighbor
could've told it.
Lucillius, I'm aging,
and still I pray for life.
Who deserves to go on,
growing old for many decades?
Many teachers are gone,
and I would abolish love
or temper it
if, sweet eros,
I knew what it really was.

Claw (RJS)

The great polymath died in the Siege
of Syracuse, where you teach, Steve.
The Roman general Marcus Claudius
Marcellus had said he should be
taken alive, though in war, as in sex,
enthusiasm can be a problem.
Tonight I make you an honorary Sicilian.
I place you at the bolt thrower—
who cares if you're blind? I'm not
asking you to kill anyone in particular.
We have better food than the Finns,
and the pine trees never play dead.
In poems, we deploy the Wise One's claw,
lifting up wooden vessels, which some call
words, and dropping them to their doom.
Our *spolia opima*? Friendship. A few rhymes.

Spread the Old Poems across Two Tables... (SK)

Titus Calpurnius Siculus,
first among Sicilian poets,
wrote eclogues
of cowherds
and country girls,
shaded groves,
sacred places,
reed pipes,
as we want spirits
to love us
and we in turn
love the world,
but weather
is changeable
and rivers swell
despite these poems.

Along the Mississippi (RJS)

Even the dead
take note when
this river swells.
They sit up—
or try to.
Being dead is
like sleeping on
a sailboat. Watch
your everlasting noggin!
And so they
do; it's almost
like watching Netflix
or SportsCenter. Almost.
In a flood,
coffins become life
buoys for others.

I'm Old Enough (SK)

To remember the itinerant
knife grinder who'd come
in his clown car
with his wheel
and hanging pots.
If you had no work
for him, he'd sit
at the curb
like Charon
waiting for his obolus.
My mother drew the curtains.
I'm old now, yes—
my first musical crush,
the Great Caruso;
my earliest toy,
brass buttons from the war.

Swallow (RJS)

I keep waiting for my son's birthmother
to show up at the door. The first year
he lived with us—he was six—she'd ride by
on her bike, but only at dusk when she
thought we couldn't see her. A little swallow
on wheels, a dart of imperfection, more
than a bit tipsy—drinking and drugs
were her unmothering—she'd pedal past.
She'd move, that is, the gears of time,
hoping for another chance. She had abused
him, of course, and he loathed her,
but nonetheless… Having just been
to Kitty Hawk, NC, I heard myself say,
with disdain, "The right mother"—as if
redemption had limits and love
were a feat that meant taking to the air.

Oh, swallow so wronged and wronging.

Notes for My Own Elegy... (SK)

I wish I could give up on sentiment,
hearing my father's voice as
he sings while driving:
"Does the spearmint lose its flavor
on the bedpost overnight?"
Wells of soft memory
overcome me,
as I, too,
near the end.
Is this how the gods call us?
My father was unkind.
My mother, a violent drunk.
I hear them now as peasants
telling good stories
under the hundred horse
chestnut trees of Sicily.

Polyps (RJS)

A note-taker as a student
and then as a scholar,
I wrote down everything—
I was serious about knowledge,
believed in it the way one believes
in a bookshelf or a set of stairs:
my fingers climbed the page...
And then one day in my fifties,
I gave myself a colonoscopy.
No directions! No Twilight!
There isn't an academic on the planet
who doesn't need a good cleaning out.
Polyps on Hegel, polyps on Marx, polyps
on the Holy Bible. What a distraction!
Read a book the way a deer
walks through snow.

Delicately.

Minatory Medicine (SK)

Reading is occult,
as Byron knew:
in the body then out
and dead grass
all around,
and the "evil eye"
sewn into his pants.
Well, you know...
Reading
is a way for us
to picture
our position
when dead.
Then our flight,
which is transitive
and curly.

Two Kinds of Dead People (RJS)

Scientists call
getting lost
in a
book "transport."
It's the
same with
death, really.
You're delivered
like a
FedEx package,
conveyed by
escalator or
moving sidewalk.
You must
get lost
to live.

Autumn (SK)

Do you remember those puffballs
in the woods—how thin
they were and
how easy to pop them?
Ego heavy, clotted,
momentum stopped,
thin ideas broken,
silly vanity...
Fate the child
who burst me
just now.
It wasn't a good day.
It's difficult to see
the comedy,
and here
come death's butterflies...

The Oldest Hackberry in Iowa City (RJS)

Enough about death.
Is there anything worse
than two old men
gumming their despair
in the barbershop of a poem?
Let me tell you about
my last erection.
It was big! It was bold!
Think: *Komodo Dragon*
of your dreams.
A veritable Monitor
of elections. I'm
voting for that peewee!
Raking up hair this morning,
which is to say leaves,
I thought, *Looking good,*

Hackberry.

Mordant Grain (SK)

Despair is all I've got,
like the shovel inside the shovel,
which declares it's innocent,
says it's just a spoon,
but even mice die
and smaller creatures.
Picture Disney dust mites
with the tiniest shovels:
Heigh Ho!
We're burying Ort
whom we loved,
who was heroic,
skating across
the president's eye,
walking on three legs.
After that…

Oar (RJS)

You've got me, babe!
Or, as a friend joked,
pretending to be
John Wilkes Booth,
"I got you, Abe."
I know, unforgivable,
but I'm trying
to make you laugh.
Paintball with words—
that's what we're
doing in this boat.
Every pun carries
a gun and, winking,
says, "Run!"
We're like clowns
in an ambulance.

Give me your oar.

9-11 (SK)

I knew people in the towers.
All day I watched TV,
feared the worst.
By nightfall I had chest pains,
started sweating.
My wife called the ambulance.
They filled me with nitro
and trundled me
to the hospital.
Was I dying?
Here came a nurse
with two hand puppets:
one, a doctor
in a white coat;
the other, Florence Nightingale.
She waved them up and down.

Iron (RJS)

Anniversaries—I hate them.
Memory rents a crane, pulls things
from the water.
A crowd, having gathered, checks its phone.
The sorting machines sigh.
"Those humans, they're at it again.
I'd rather they were demented.
It would be more fitting, more honest."
"Shut the hell up," says the crane.
"What do you expect of a creature
who must dash into the present?
They're like dogs—that's where they're fed.
We, on the other hand, are made
of iron; we marvel at our rust
and endure, brittle though
we may be."

Crows (SK)

Quick, what's the difference between
a crow and a crane?
OK. Don't bother.
No one names machines
after corvids.
Once I lived
on "Andy the Raven Street,"
but that was long ago.
What I mean is
Raven Street
was the most ordinary place
with its cement dwellings
and bus stops. What I mean
is the street was unnatural,
like a gaunt man of the imagination
who flaps his wings at twilight.

Again (RJS)

I lost twenty pounds when I had
that hole in my colon. My sigmoid colon,
to be precise. For those who get
lost in the body, it's the part closest
to the rectum. Think of it as the exit
at City Field: the crowds leaving
en masse, as red as a Cardinal
though their team is blue. Yes,
I was bleeding—profusely, I might add.
A gaunt man of the hospital,
in need of iron. The doctor, beefy
as a kielbasa, a frat bro (Alpha Sigma
Phi), a butcher of names, approached,
and before he got there said,
his voice thundering down the hall,
"Mr. Snarvarese, I need to look

at your anus again."

Throat, Concluding with a Line from Livy (SK)

They put a string with meat on it
right down the gullet, mine,
hoping to find out
why I was starving myself —
surely no teen,
certainly no boy,
would hit 96 pounds
on purpose;
surely some ravening juice
in the abdominal cave
was bleaching the child.
So, they held me,
pushed cooked veal
into the hatch—
"We can endure neither
our vices nor their cure."

More to Me (RJS)

I told him I would be landing planes
at O'Hare during the surgery—
I'm that hypervigilant— if he didn't double
the recommended dose of anesthesia.
"Your eyes see a 155-pound man," I said,
"but my nervous system is triple that."
"We want you to wake up," he replied.
"Yes, but not *during* the procedure."

Doctors never listen. First thing I *saw*...
Blood was everywhere; he had just
cut an inch off my femur. And then
the lightning mice of pain... Steve,
let's invent a new kind of stethoscope.
Like Trump in his tower, my heart
is tired of being spied upon.
There's more to me than my heart!

III

From a Lecture (SK)

Skaldic verse, allusions to mythology,
numerous fragments of tales,
lists of alternative poetic terms
for a wide range of things,
including supernatural entities
(such as the many names of Odin).
But I say doctors also,
Thor's servants
with this hammer
and that bellows,
a draft of leaden malt,
pretending they can
lift your dying friend
atop the piled stones,
ringing the doctor bells,
poking fingers into smoke...

Once When I Was Drunk (RJS)

Lose some weight if you
want me to lift you.
I will do the same.
Even in grief, a bad
back is a bad back.
As a child I thought Ben
Gay was Ben Hur—
chariots and muscles,
each of them pulled...
Once when I was drunk,
I reached for a tube
and brushed my teeth.
My gums were gladiators,
and my mouth, the Coliseum.
Let us both say a prayer
for fallen warriors.

Monster (SK)

He is a man of perfect charm and fascination. A monster, in
short.—Gore Vidal on Aaron Burr

Look at the monster:
Lusus naturae
with shiny American teeth.
He says you're alive.
Open your eyes—
he's shabby, asymmetrical,
like a Roman Emperor
in drag, how does one
say it in short?
Big emotions signal value,
so he brings little ones.
Reductive sexualization
of the mind, baby envies,
pseudo-religion
of self-centeredness,
but what a smile...

Defaulted (RJS)

This is truffle season / Tom Ford tuxedos
for no reason. —Jay Z

We've gone a whole book
without epigraphs. You fucker!
And now this poem must dress up,
put on a tuxedo. A book,
I guess, is a ball. Once,
playing tennis, my opponent
hit me in the mouth with his racket.
I had kindly leaned over the net
to pick up the Dacron orb—the kid,
while a dick, seemed dejected—
and when I rose, a dove with pockets,
I had flown into wood.
"Greetings, Jack Kramer!"
My tooth turned black as the devil:
a little coffin in my mouth,
a minor key on a stunned piano.

Getting Away with It (SK)

Reading quotes about tennis is
a misericordia—no one's worse
than David Foster Wallace.
But I digress, the subject
is the grandest of topics,
the Limitations of Kindness.
Van Eyck: "As I can
But not as I would."
Parse empathy,
think twice.
Can you be kind
is the question?
Let your stomach
be your guide.
It digests many
a spoiled thing.

Underspin (RJS)

In "Tennis, the Menace," an episode of *The Simpsons,* Grandpa
wins a talent show at the Springfield Retirement Castle. His prize:
a free autopsy. So that he may be fully prepared for the future,
his grandson Homer buys him a casket and tombstone. Speaking
to a salesman, he discovers that a certain type of tombstone
contains the same amount of cement as a tennis court. Tennis and
death—the link, as a judge might say, is *material.* Homer then
decides to build a court, though he hasn't played much tennis
before. He's terrible. American tennis stars Sampras, Agassi,
and the Williams sisters rescue him by holding an exhibition.
Recovering his pride, Homer secretly lightens the wallet of Pistol
Pete and with that windfall takes his family to dinner. Call this
poem a plot summary: the words like dirt, the racket a shovel. Once,
at the White House, Ronald Reagan joked, "I was going to take
up tennis until I found out you couldn't get the horse on the court."
Which is how I feel about David Foster Wallace, that lumbering,

overwrought sad-ass who couldn't get the novel there either.

I Don't Care for Rilke (SK)

Sometimes I leave home
because of crickets,
blackbirds,
clouds like cats
following, a few strangers
now and then.
I walk
for miles, trees
translating wind
with no mention
of sports,
or junk mail,
presidents,
crying coins,
musical scores
and baseballs.

Spared (RJS)

Thanks for playing catch, Steve.
It's dark. The sky's meowing.
Even my mitt is hungry…
To the stove I say, "How about
burning something for the two of us?"
To the wine, "Don't just stand there!"
To myself, "You need a new edition."
Who was it who quipped, "Translation
is like travel"? Whenever an original
passes through customs, loss is declared.
After the sky, let's translate the aspen,
its green-going-to-yellow.
Tonight I simply have to do laundry.
Without color-guard detergent,
my t-shirts will fade. On one, Nixon
is bowling. No one is spared.

You Can't Use the Word "Longing" in Poetry Anymore... (SK)

But leaves fall.
They whirl under street-lamps,
"Death's butterflies,"
as my friend Jarkko
called them—and
he's gone, too.
Try talking about life
without clean desire,
also known
as tenderness—also
called yearning,
aching, pining,
and for what?
The day held meaning,
we felt accomplished,
we swept the children's hair.

Gust (RJS)

But men rise—
if not from the ground,
then from bed,
that unmade flower,
that petunia of the sheets.
Or from the dinner table,
which looks like
the ground if you squint.
Or the sofa, slick
casket of immobility.
Men rise the way
leaves do in autumn.
A sudden gust—
call it spirit; call
it second thoughts.
"I'm not done falling,"
say these monarchs
of wind.

Fuck Disney (SK)

Everyone wants to be king.
So, they sell King Size beds,
socks "fit for a King."
There's "King of the jungle,"
Bob Marley, "Reggae King."
Very few resist—
no one asks for
"Regicide sized coffee"
or a dram
of Jefferson's wine.
They wish to rise
from inside flowers,
pollinated grief
in their hair,
a mantilla of envy
only a crown can cover.

Distinctions (RJS)

Once in a poem
about John Milton, I wrote,
The regicides were hung.
The editor of a literary journal
scribbled in the margin,
"Delighted to learn this.
How big were their
codpieces?"
"What a dick!" I said
to myself. Meaning:
he's the king.
Meaning: *he will die*
one way
or another.
Gallows and cock.
Hanged and hung.

Of Course You Meant "Hung
Like Harry Reems"… (SK)

But you can't expect the average poetry editor
to know a cod piece from a damp squib
or to tell the difference
between a fizzled firework
and a short literary composition
of a satirical
or sarcastic character.
I think of Pound:
"Man reading should be man intensely alive.
The book should be a ball of light in one's hand."
Hung like Ezra is a sinister simile—
"Speak against unconscious oppression,
speak against the tyranny of the unimaginative,
speak against bonds."
BTW: before he got on camera,
Harry worked for the lighting crew.

He Wanted to Be on Broadway (RJS)

I had a friend who worked at a center for the performing arts.
He took tickets, showed old ladies to their seats.
One kissed him on the mouth; one puckered and plunged.
(Besotted arrow, tipped with need, stumbling on its path...)
A third, like a Delta Force commando, landed
in the compound of his pocket and felt him up—
later, he discovered a hundred-dollar bill.
Minks and loneliness.

One Saturday, the lighting guy was out sick.
Dolly Parton had arrived—her breasts like a presidential
advance team—and he would have to fill in.
He would have to man the followspot,
friend of prison guards and theatre techs.
In his ear, whenever he strayed, a command: "Light the money!"
Years later, having made no progress on his dream,
he drew a cartoon. Added a single letter to the punchline:

"Blight the money! Blight the money!"

How It Is... (SK)

Saarikoski told me by phone
we'd meet sometime
in this mad world,
which was gentle
given his imminent
death—his knowing.
(I was young,
not yet thirty.)
He was
drinking himself
to death. Autumn,
a strict season:
leaves falling,
saying
we'll meet sometime
in the coming madness.

Gud (RJS)

He hadn't won the Nobel yet,
but he was famous,
and I, a fledgling poet,
had been chosen to introduce him.
Imagine the sorriest of shepherds —
I had no published sheep! —
introducing God,
who was on a book tour,
his Ten Commandments
having become a best seller.
First things first: get his name right.
It's not Gad or Ged or Gud.
It's God, as in cod, as in great bod, God!
My tongue turned Seamus to Shemus
and Heaney to Haynie.
Off-rhymes of himself, dyslexic,
sinning in sound...

More About Gud (SK)

He has no temple,
but once
I found myself
among his faithful
"furries"
holding a convention
in my hotel:
pink fox,
leather bear,
limping hippo,
rubbing and grinding
in the elevators,
and me
with a guide dog.
They followed us down the hall,
calling for absolutions...

Parishioners (RJS)

I wish Gud would retire,
hand over his hand
to someone else,
anyone really:
my neighbor the asshole,
my neighbor the drunk,
my neighbor the Weed Wacker,
my neighbor the toke…

When I say anyone,
I mean anyone.
It's like electing the Orange Man:
pull the lever in a daze.
Gad, ged, gud…
In every mouth
a votive candle.
Who can blame

the parishioners?

What Makes You Think... (SK)

OK, look, when you're drunk in foreign cities,
you see stars are also under our feet.
Warsaw, Tivoli, Kingston,
Gud is down there,
and like a game of Twister
all you've got to do
is put your clompers
on the right dots.
Gud is the superstitious ink
known to Luther
but with less heart
than even the Lutherans
could conceive.
He's a block of wood
with eyes,
fits under any drunk's shoe.

Wet Monday (RJS)

For Michael Hofmann

I had traveled to Torun, in north-central Poland,
on what a Polish friend of mine called—
he was learning English—the Fistula Raver.
Day after Easter. Hailstones and pestilence.
An old woman, three stories up,
dropped a bucket of water on me.
Then some kids attacked with water guns.
How was I supposed to know about *Lany
Poniedziałek*? It's a custom dating back
to the 14th century in which boys
from the countryside lash girls with pussy willows.
Meaning: *I will marry you later*. I took
refuge in the cathedral, thought of Copernicus,
who was born in Torun, as the shrieking
moved around me like an astral body.
At dusk I passed the Museum of Gingerbread.

One More Poem About Drinking in Foreign Locales (SK)

This isn't about me;
it's not one of those stories.
I did however see a man
talking gently to a statue
one night
in London,
his earnestness
a thing of alchemical
beauty,
as if he, too,
had been a rose,
a bull or
became Europa;
had loved
the queen—
keeping her alive...

Broom (RJS)

We weren't drinking,
but we were playing tennis
illegally—or at least without invitation.
The red clay court in Bratislava
was immaculate—freshly swept,
the lines like a dental patient
who's just received
a good cleaning.
The court smiled at us.
It said, "Please kiss me."
We'd only hit a backhand or two
before that battle-axe
came at us with a broom.
A statue of sorts, one my friend
spoke Russian to, forgetting
all about the Prague Spring.

When the Statues Come to Life… (SK)

Every clotted child knows it's bad—
Frosty the Snowman,
just another perv uncle.
Worse, the dancing ones,
Colonel Snap-tooth,
down from his plinth.
Even the good ones,
Helen Keller
following you home
on granite legs
will scare the shit
out of you, stunt
your growth,
which is why
I'm short, Madame Blavatsky,
so fucking short.

Theosophy (RJS)

Helena Petrovna called them
"Masters of Ancient Wisdom,"
spiritual adepts who offered
guidance and sometimes instruction.
They sent her, she said, to Shigatse,
Tibet where she earned (I'm making
this up) a degree in counseling.
Knowledge was an unhappy family—
everyone estranged. Father
philosophy, mother religion,
and that bastard child science.
Oh, the bickering! For centuries,
the adepts had behaved like air
traffic controllers, keeping the planes
apart. Now they wanted them to collide.
Madame Blavatsky flu, let us say,

before her time.

Helena Petrovna... (SK)

Who's dirty?
Bad God!
Try not to touch anything!
Walk everywhere while glowing.
When you're pure spirit,
it can't be helped.
What to do
with your shoes, honey?
Angel socks,
mesmer gloves—
holy hatpins.
Love this game!
Yes, Paris is medieval.
Fief d'Alby, Grand Court of Miracles,
and you my dear, pretending also!

There's More Dignity in Being a Terrorist (RJS)

For nearly two months I heard music
coming from my leg: feint songs with lyrics
I recognized—*Brandy, you're a fine girl*—
muffled by muscle and bone.
I told no one, not even my wife.
How do you ask a woman to listen to your leg?
"Oh, yes," said the orthopedist, "your hip
replacement is acting like an antenna.
You're picking up things."
The boon my disability friends talk about!
The music of walking in another way!
Literally! Once, at a TSA checkpoint,
the band inside me set off an alarm.
"I have a hip replacement," I said.
"Aren't you a little young?" the agent replied.
When he discovered I was telling the truth,

pity became his wand.

Blind Reception 1966 (SK)

Radio, my best pal.
Disabled, lonesome,
shut away
(how they like it
in America).
WPTR 1540,
a pure accommodation:
"50,000 Watts
of Rock & Roll!"
A pompadoured disc jockey,
"Boom Boom Branigan,"
my Svengali—
I was Trilby
hypnotized,
moving my lips,
almost a singer.

Housewife (RJS)

With hypnosis, too, there are
believers and unbelievers:
the altered state proponents,
the nonstate proponents—
the latter like any
demystifying force.
Placebo effect, imaginative
role enactment...
From the Greek for "nervous sleep,"
a paradoxical form of concentration.
Monoideism, that lone angel
on the head of a pin.
The rest, you could say, is mist.
When my mother tried to give up
smoking, she promptly
hid all the silverware.

Lobster (SK)

Did you know you can hypnotize lobsters?
It's true. And dogs. Sure, your mother.
My mother ate fire, and only pills
did the trick, Valhalla in Walla Walla,
Mumsy go poof! Meanwhile
in the attic, playing with
my chemistry set,
I made cloud-people
who rose to heaven
quickly and
without suggestion.
Particulate
creation knows
what to do,
which means
Freud's patients were…?

Oh, No, DFW Again (RJS)

Lobsters are like footnotes:
they lurk at the bottom
where everything clouds,
and readers go to die.
Every footnote has an exoskeleton,
a chitinous carapace.
When you boil a footnote,
it turns orange.
(Think of Republicans turning Trump.)
They're blue-blooded, like spiders and snails;
it's not so much the hemocyanin,
which contains copper,
as their devotion to exclusivity.
Footnotes are always fair-skinned royals.
"Consider the lobster's pain," says DFW.
I say, "What about the reader's?"

Trap (SK)

Of course DFW stands for Department
of Fish and Wildlife.
Poetry always says
we're smarter than we knew.
We were homesick at first,
then we found true Ithaca.
"True Ithaca" might
be the title of a good poem.
Please write it.
Back to the fish
and wildlife—
the American lobster
was thought
to be a poor man's food.
A meal, like a poem,
begins as a lump in the throat.

Ledge (RJS)

It's not "True Ithaca," Steve,
but Iowa City is fine,
hardly an island—
an island maybe
of progressive thought.
(In this election season,
Joni Ernst beguiles
the cornfields; her hair
screams, "Detassel me.")
It was better when you
lived here, when we
could send poems
by homing pigeon,
right to the ledge
of the other's
heart.

IV

Bag Man, Iowa City (SK)

Everyone needs one
film noir, shifty,
threadbare coat,
packing money
and stolen watches—
in this case,
your past
so clear
you can't blink it
away, as when
he pulls from his pocket
Suzy's brassiere
with a rose
stitched
between
its cups.

Supernumerary (RJS)

Someone on Facebook
asked for poems about
women's breasts. Diane
Seuss said she couldn't
bear to read any by men,
so, Ralph, be careful.
(I often talk to myself
when discussing the body.)
Breasts are oppressed,
I get it, but I got some
myself—in fact, I have
three. The extra's called
a supernumerary nipple.
Google says it's a birth
defect. A birth defect!
It exists on the milk line,

and suckles my dreams.

Now and Then... (SK)

I wish for a third ear,
wanting to catch
what Rachmaninov
caught in wind,
and certainly
a third nostril
to catch pepper
and roasting lamb
from the next
village. I'll bring
the vodka,
raising it
with my third
hand and cry out
like Chaliapin
under a massive clock.

At the Movies (RJS)

As a boy, I loved *Good & Plenty*—
now they just pull out my fillings.
Little grave diggers in reverse,
exhuming a dental coffin. My sibling
said, "They're fetuses in snow."
Another said, "They're saintly turds."
We were bored; the previews hadn't
yet begun; darkness made us brave
with mischief. I said, "They're astronauts
in capsules who must sleep for
a hundred years"—it takes forever
to get to the next star system.
One by one, the candy passed through
the heliopause, the box like solar wind
diminishing. Ahead: termination shock,
14 billion kilometers from my tongue.

Pluto, I assure you, is a planet.

You Have to Choose... (SK)

Candy is pain disguised,
like the game we played
with a wallet on a string.
The old man bends
and we'd
tug his fortune.
No reason
to expect joy,
but the young
and old
fall for it.
You've got to
believe in something,
and why not,
you know,
buy a goddamned big car?

Heehawing (RJS)

Gallo's humor—that's
what my mother called
the liquid rope heehawing
that wine affords.
Through a glass darkly,
she would joke,
or several glasses…
Why not the whole bottle?

She loved Necco Wafers.
They were like swallowing chalk,
a calculating blackboard.
Pretty in pink does math!
She used to help me
with my calculus homework
while making dinner.
"Slow down, Mom, I don't

understand."

Leaves Blow through the Halls… (SK)

When Odysseus came home
and killed the suitors,
Homer says they scattered
like dead leaves.
Or so I recall it—
the point is
the world went faster,
the mind was quickened
when the arrow
passed through
the line of axes.
Numbers had changed,
Athena went Boolean.
No discrete set
for horny freeloaders—
if x is false, then the value of y can be ignored…

The Problem with Mythology (RJS)

A baker will say
of yeast or of dough,
"It proves so well"—
as if it were Odysseus
and rising were
as much a test
as a revelation,
even a kind of *fait accompli.*
Call the proving oven
trial by fire or
at least by heat.
I am who I am:
the crust of tautology.
So this is what
"Honey, I'm home!"
means.

The World before Eclairs or Odysseus (SK)

Forget Lars Gustafsson
and the world before Bach—
when I was three,
I loved a certain bakery
in Paris, *la ficille*,
the string loaf,
so my parents
had to buy me
bread-as-toy.
bread as whip.
bread le rabat.
You could
beat the bushes
with it,
as I did
waving from my *pliage* stroller...

1990 (RJS)

In Poznan, I grew tired of beets. I loathed them
the way I loathed former party officials
in the period before lustracja. "Borscht is an evil bastard,"
I would say, "a real asshole! Screw you, Borscht."
He got his job—and his place at the table—unfairly.
The dream of full employment should not extend
to deadbeets. No kiss-ass commies, please.
And the whole bleeding red act—give me a break.
What a time! Russian pasta fell apart like dissidents
"in the hospital." Snow accumulated on the windowsill
inside. The head of the English Institute
had been Minister of Education under Jaruzelski,
imprisoning some of his colleagues during Martial Law.
(Don't tell me about your problematic department.)
Walking home, I'd see women beeting their rugs
and men, their potatoes. Vegetal apostrophe—

it's as satisfying as challah or braided egg *chleb*.

Peloponnese Taverna 1977 (SK)

I ate sheep's head soup,
all the while
telling others
about Kuru, the long drop
into torpor,
a desire to eat
your arms off,
though not right away.
I assured them
it'd take decades—
they'd be bankers,
women senators
when they'd become incontinent,
but not before gibbering,
the sponge-like holes
in their brains widening like gyres...

Riser (RJS)

Steve, your poems
are like a set of stairs—
some missing, some
messing with the riser.
A funhouse of longing,
the bedrooms all budrooms:
dahlias refusing
to say hi
and then, in an instant,
splayed like roadkill
on the hi-way.
Every bee will fuck them.
(That's not nice!)
Every florist will weep.
Tonight let's all
eat color.

Pup Canto (SK)

Dogs know roadkill from a world
before roads—
back when rats could off themselves
from medieval despair
(outrunning the plague etc.).
But no dog would screw
a dahlia as you say.
I've always known they're sinister,
the bees— with their powdered dances,
jellied deaths in the hive.
They gossip also:
Bzzzz. Queen Hortense
sneaks out
to sleep in octopoidal
flowers...Bzzz
Bzzz.

Loehmann's (RJS)

My mother, Queen Hortense, hated
dressing rooms (she already felt trapped
by marriage), and so she'd make us try
on clothes in the display area—next
to the mannequins who braved their exposure
so much better than we did. (Think of them
as arctic explorers, icy winds having made them British,
which is to say rigid, which is to say dead.)
"Off! Off!" my mother would shout,
meaning pants, meaning shirt,
meaning *I don't have time for this!*
How we all didn't end up as nudists
or predatory priests escapes me.
My mother, on the other hand, would shop
for hours at Loehmann's while we kids
waited in the car, pulling each other's hair

like a church bell.

Jordan Marsh, etc. (SK)

Once I had diarrhea in Jordan Marsh,
the flagship one in Boston,
and once I got lost in Macy's
when I climbed aboard
the up escalator
and my parents never saw.
Once I stole a mannequin's nose
in Sibley's and once
a detective followed me
in Montgomery Ward
since I looked like a hippie
by then. Once I bought birds
in Woolworth's
to release them.
Once I bought roller skates
blind, just to circle the aisles.

Profound (RJS)

You had to mention diarrhea—
from the Greek for "through"
and "flow." (Picture the Holland Tunnel,
backed up at rush hour and then…)
Secretory, osmotic, exudative—
I know my diarrheas!
They might as well be dogbane,
and my bowels, a working greenhouse!
Oh, the delightful smell. Squirt, Squirt.
Diarrhea has a purpose.
Scientists speak of an "evolved
expulsion defense mechanism."
Shit as a fighter pilot who simply
must leave his plane. Now!
Don't let anyone tell you
toilet humor isn't profound.

From the Greek (SK)

They don't say you've overdone it,
but instead you've over-shit them,
reminding me
of a high school pal
who bragged
he'd shat
in a church pew,
and I said
lovingkindness
comes in many guises,
but he didn't get it.
For him it was contempt,
but already
I knew divine over-shit.
Skata sta moutra sou…
Shit in your face.

Due (RJS)

Church pews turned into stretchers
after that Palm Sunday tornado
struck in Alabama. Why shouldn't
they provide this sort of salvation, too?
The problem with religion? It operates
like binary code: Xs *or* Os; bodies *or* souls.
When ripped from the floor, a pew has
many options, many possible lives.
It's like a college graduate: a stage,
a speech, black hats in the air…
Vacillate all you want; it won't help.
In Gainesville, Florida, I met a man who
bought an old EMT truck and reworked
the lettering: AMBIVALENCE VEHICLE.
None of us becomes what we want.
We make do. We come due.

Tinker Bell (SK)

Like Arial she's inside the tree,
inside the stave, lance,
inside the bleacher,
the pew, the ghastly pew.
Tinker Bell, dear thing,
light of innocence
locked up,
Dickensian,
buried alive
in wood.
No wonder you think
with such rectitude
about the next life
when sitting in church.
The wood nymph shining
a light up your ass.

Wings (RJS)

"You silly ass"—that is Tinker Bell's
favorite insult in the musical version
of *Peter Pan*. When she's mad,
she's mad; when she's amused,
she's amused. A fairy's size
apparently prevents her from feeling
more than one emotion at once.
So much for poetry. So much
for adulthood. The only time I feel
one thing exclusively is when I'm in
a faculty meeting. Then, sure, give me
some pixie dust and a Claritin.
A man named Malcolm surrenders
his son and becomes Peter Pan.
Wings for a child. Listen up, Malcolm,
I adopted your boy, wresting him

from the Shadow.

Admission (SK)

I threw Tinker Bell
down the well
for Timmy and Lassie
to find while the big boys,
doing a man's work,
are busy dismembering
themselves
with power equipment,
as Robert Frost
told us, and fuck
Tinker Bell,
floating down there
with rodent skulls
and bed springs
and solid, discarded
American teeth.

The Anti-Vaxxers Are at It Again (RJS)

She was a mender
of pots and kettles
who spoke the language of bells.
There was jealousy in
every pinprick of sound,
the woods a doctor
administering vaccinations.
TB stands for…
All you need is faith,
trust and a little bit
of pixie dust.
Hogwash!
She's an American gnat—
oh, whining fatuity!—
a mosquito
of the lowest order.

Pass the Plasma, Dolley Madison (SK)

Here's my arm, a leg really.
We're all walking on our hands
in America, sweating,
hoping carnival tricks
will keep us or kill us.
Did you see that woman
in the newspaper
wearing a sign—
"I'd rather my family is dead
than live in fear of COVID"?
O Dolley, disaffection
surrounds us—
pack up the china,
cut the paintings
from their frames.
Messengers bid us fly...

Fists (RJS)

Route 123, Dolley Madison Boulevard, in McLean, VA.
It's how you get to my childhood home on the Potomac

and to the CIA. Remember the shooting in 1993, right
there at the entrance? Mir Qazi killed two employees

who were waiting to turn into the facility. One was
an agent; the other, a doctor who divined the health

of foreign leaders. Qazi escaped but was later captured,
rendered, and executed. Competing monuments praise

the martyrs: a granite wall with benches, and a mosque
in the port city of Ormara. Dolley would have asked

the monuments to tea, believing that fists are no match
for cake. She is said, by historians, to have given birth

to bipartisanship. In August of 1793, yellow fever found
Philadelphia hiding in a closet. It killed 5,000 people in

just four months. Dolley lost her first husband, John Todd,
her infant son, William, and her parents-in-law. Fists

or cake?

Fists or Cake (SK)

This is the American question.
Even when cattle
stood no taller than today's
small dogs, the Anglo-Scott-French
setting foot—here—as it were
would rather fight than fuck.
There are no quotes
about settlers and cake.
Corpses, recipes,
spent ammunition—
there are sayings:
gonna get some tail
meant beaver tail,
roasted for fatty texture
and gamey flavor.
No cakes for miles.

Vespucci (RJS)

It's as if the rain were
a trapper: it pelts
the roof.
What a sad tale:
the beaver in America.
We cover our heads
one way or another—
wood, fur—until
fashion changes
or we deplete the resource.
When we went upright,
when we set foot
until there was no place
without prints, no paws...
Daniel Boone
was a goon.

Cibo (SK)

I like to order the Vespucci
when I'm dining out
with clams
alle vongole!
When the haughty
Milanese waiter
refuses to give me
shredded parmesan
with a moue of disgust,
I climb on the table,
strike an attitude
and shout:
I'm from America!
I'm the descendent
of all your appetites.
Salt and freshly ground pepper to taste…

Give Passion Its Due (RJS)

I've seen exactly this:
you mounting the table
like a horse, shouting
expletives in Finnish…
The first time we ate
sushi together—was it
1561?—you said,
"Order for me." And I did.
The little rolls like strait-
jackets, the chopsticks
like Puritan trees. Even
the sake seemed composed.
We both prefer Italian.
Who needs a gun when
you have gravy? Dinner is
always a bloodbath.

What If (SK)

We could make meals last for days,
as with the Florentine Pogen?
Silvered oysters,
sabres under the benches,
houses of the poor
tumbling down
our gullets,
savory-villages
straight down our throats.
For what else
are meals for
but conquest
and social ruin?
Oh Pogen,
there's a dead man
behind this forcella...

Spoons (RJS)

Christine Miserandino is at a diner with a friend
who asks, "What is Lupus like?" Taking spoons
from an adjacent table, she turns the utensil
into a unit of energy. Each activity of the day,
whether it is loved or loathed, requires a spoon.
Dressing: spoon. Teaching a class: spoon. Shopping:
spoon. Doing laundry: spoon. Even sex with your
partner: spoon. There are no forks in this economy.
The spoons have become knives, rusty ones that
cause Tetanus. The spoons daily put a fork in it.
It's like rationing in a war: you may have only three
small pieces of cheese. You may teach but not get
dressed; you may fuck but not have clean clothes.
The word "stamina" comes from "thread" in Latin,
as in threads spun by the Fates. Your sweater,
like your life, is unraveling.

More about Spoons (SK)

I found a spoon in the snow
outside Rochester, NY,
right beside the Erie Canal.
Oh it was old alright.
Like the suicide necktie
one buys at Goodwill.
The snow spoon
rusted like your mother's
memories—
those were good times,
she'd say—
when carried
in my pocket
became a life
inside a life,
a worm inside a thistle.

Angel (RJS)

Why does silver
need to be polished
and pewter, beaten
into beauty?
Yes, the brave dress up
for death. It's like
a concert when you're young.
Starch is not your friend,
but it does keep time—
steals it, in fact.
Every child is a minor
chord, and every
parent, a pedal.
Sustain, sustain, sustain…
When the music stops,
it lies down

in the snow.

Biographies

Stephen Kuusisto directs The Burton Blatt Institute's Research Programs in disability at Syracuse University where he holds a University Professorship. He is the author of the memoirs *Planet of the Blind* (a New York Times "Notable Book of the Year") and *Eavesdropping: A Memoir of Blindness and Listening* and of the poetry collections *Only Bread, Only Light, Letters to Borges*, and *Old Horse, What Is To Be Done?* His newest memoir, *Have Dog, Will Travel: A Poet's Journey* is new from Simon & Schuster. A graduate of the Iowa Writer's Workshop and a Fulbright Scholar, he has taught at the University of Iowa, Hobart & William Smith Colleges, and The Ohio State University. Kuusisto has served as an advisor to the Metropolitan Museum and the Museum of Modern Art in New York and the National Endowment for the Arts in Washington, DC and has appeared on numerous television and radio programs including The Oprah Winfrey Show; Dateline; All Things Considered; Morning Edition; Talk of the Nation; A & E; and Animal Planet. His essays have appeared in *The New York Times; The Washington Post; Harper's; The Reader's Digest*; and his daily blog "Planet of the Blind" is read globally by people interested in disability and contemporary culture.

Ralph James Savarese is the author of two books of prose, *Reasonable People: A Memoir of Autism and Adoption* and *See It Feelingly: Classic Novels, Autistic Readers, and the Schooling of a No-Good English Professor*, and two volumes of poetry, *Republican Fathers* and *When This Is Over: Pandemic Poems*. He has also co-edited three collections, including the first on the concept of neurodiversity. His work has appeared, among other places, in *American Poetry Review*, *Bellingham Review*, *Beloit Poetry Journal*, *Modern Poetry in Translation*, *Mudlark*, *New England Review*, *Nine Mile Magazine*, *Ploughshares*, *Rogue Agent*, *Seneca Review*, *Sewanee Review*, *Southern Humanities Review*, *Southern Poetry Review*, *Southwest Review*, and *Wordgathering*. He has appeared in three documentaries about autism, including his son's, *Deej*, which appeared on PBS and won a Peabody Award. He teaches at Grinnell College and lives in Iowa City, IA.